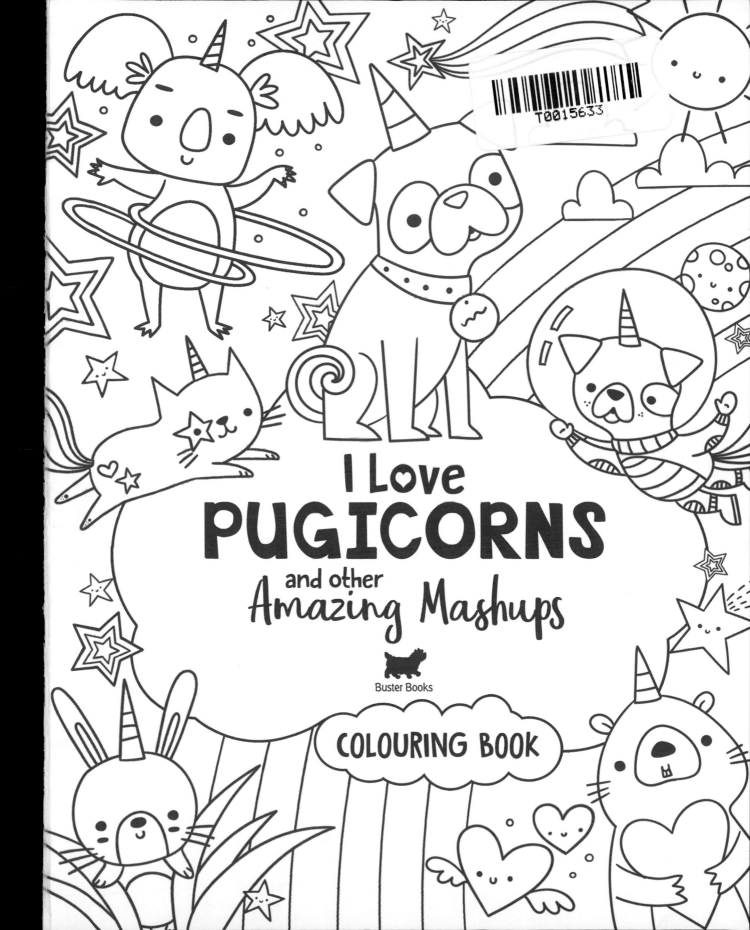

I Love
PUGICORNS
and other
Amazing Mashups

Buster Books

COLOURING BOOK

First published in Great Britain in 2022 by Buster Books,
an imprint of Michael O'Mara Books Limited, 9 Lion Yard,
Tremadoc Road, London SW4 7NQ

W www.mombooks.com/buster   F Buster Books   T @BusterBooks   I @buster_books

Copyright © Buster Books 2022

ISBN: 978-1-78055-810-3

2 4 6 8 10 9 7 5 3 1

This book was printed in March 2022 by Bell & Bain Ltd,
303 Burnfield Road, Thornliebank, Glasgow,
G46 7UQ, United Kingdom.

FSC
www.fsc.org

MIX
Paper from
responsible sources
FSC® C007785

Illustrated by Sarah Wade

Edited by Josephine Southon
Designed by Jade Moore
Cover Design by Angie Allison

Sparkle like a pugicorn.

Fly high, little
slothicorn.

Good times only
at this pugicorn party.

This is one VIP
(Very Important Poodlecorn).

Believe in a bunnicorn.

Grow your own way,
little llamacorn.

Live your life in a
pandacorn paradise.

Leave a sprinkle of magic wherever you go.

Follow your own
purrfect caticorn path.

Yummy pupsicles and caticookies every day.

Keep calm and
koalacorn.

Once upon a
pupcorn party.

Shine bright like
a unicorn.

Otterly obsessed.

Ride the waves and
go with the flow.

Find joy in the
little things.

A little sunshine goes
a long way.

Anything is pawsible.

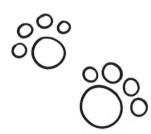

Don't worry, be puppy.

Life is sweet and so are you.

In a world of siestas,
find the fiestas.

Every day is
a new adventure.

These boots were
made for dreaming.

Be a slothicorn and create your own rainbows.

50% koala,
50% unicorn,
100% fabulous.

All you need is ice cream
... and a little imagination.

Make a wish and keep
on dreaming.

Live the llamacorn
dream.

No one's raining on this puppy's parade.

Reach for the stars.